Contents

What are trees?

Trees are plants. Some trees are the biggest and tallest plants in the world. There is an amazing variety of trees and they can look very different from each other. All trees have a woody **trunk** that gives them their height and strength. Many trees produce flowers, or blossom, in spring or summer.

These Redwood trees can reach a height of 113 metres.

Tree Fact

There are trees alive today that are more than 4,000 years old.

See how plants grow
Trees

Nicola Edwards

7000354015

WAYLAND

Copyright © Wayland 2006

Published in Great Britain in 2006 by Wayland,
a division of Hachette Children's Books

This paperback edition published in 2008 by
Wayland.

Editor: Penny Worms
Senior Design Manager: Rosamund Saunders
Designer: Elaine Wilkinson

Wayland,
338 Euston Road
London NW1 3BH

All rights reserved. Apart from any use permitted
under UK copyright law, this publication may only
be reproduced, stored or transmitted, in any form,
or by any means with prior permission in writing
of the publishers or in the case of reprographic
production in accordance with the terms of
licences issued by the Copyright Licensing Agency.

British Library Cataloguing in Publication Data
Edwards, Nicola
        Trees. - (See how they grow)
        1. Trees - Juvenile literature
        I. Title
        582.1'6

ISBN 9780750255875

Printed in China

Wayland is a division of Hachette Children's
Books, an Hachette Livre UK company.

www.hachettechildrens.co.uk

WORCESTERSHIRE
COUNTY COUNCIL

150

Bertrams | 29/01/2009

J582.16 | £6.99

BV

The publishers would like to thank the following
for allowing us to reproduce their pictures in
this book:
Alamy: 5 (Steve Bly). Corbis images: 8 (Wes
Thompson), 10 (Richard Cummins), 12
(L. Clarke), 14 (Doug Wilson), 16 (Wolfgang
Flamisch), 23 (Robert Estall). Ecoscene: title page
and 13 (Chinch Gryniewicz), 4 (Sally Morgan),
9 (Nicholas & Sherry Lu Aldridge), 18 (Kjell
Sandved), 20 (Chinch Gryniewicz), 21 (Chinch
Gryniewicz). Getty images: 7 (Luca Trovato),
11 (Muntz), 17 (Craig Line), 19 (K & K
Ammann). Photolibrary: cover and 6 (Ian West).
Wayland Picture Library: 15, 22.

How many different types of trees can you see in this picture?

Where do trees grow?

Trees grow everywhere. See how many different trees you can spot in your local area. Some trees grow along the sides of roads or on banks at the edges of motorways. People plant trees in their gardens. Your local park may have trees that are hundreds of years old.

▶ The branches of a tree grow wider when they have space to spread out.

◀ There have probably been **palm trees** growing on this beach for hundreds of years.

Trees around the world

Trees grow all over the world. They can survive in very cold, snowy areas and grow on steep mountain slopes.
In **tropical rainforests** where it is hot and wet, trees crowd together.

▼ Eucalyptus trees grow in areas where there is little rain. Their leaves provide food for koalas.

In dry areas, trees grow far apart as their **roots** struggle to get enough water.

▼ Mangrove trees grow in swamps full of salty sea water.

Types of trees

There are three main groups of trees: palm trees, **conifers** and **broadleaved trees**. Palms have slim trunks and tough, waterproof leaves. They produce fruit such as dates and coconuts.

▼ In autumn, the leaves of broadleaved trees change colour and fall off. The tree grows new leaves in spring.

Conifers such as pine trees have thin, spiny, needle-like leaves. **Cones** grow on these trees. Broadleaved trees have wide, flat leaves and they produce flowers and fruit.

▼ The fir trees we decorate at Christmas are conifers.

The parts of a tree

Like all plants, a tree has roots that hold it in the ground and soak up water and **nutrients**. The trunk is a **stem** covered in a layer of **bark**. Bark protects the trunk and helps to stop the tree losing water.

branch

trunk

roots

▶ Roots spread out underground and hold the tree firmly in the soil.

Branches and twigs grow like arms and fingers from the trunk. **Buds** form on the twigs and grow into leaves and sometimes flowers.

▼ Acorns are the fruit of an oak tree.

acorn

leaf

Tree Fact

Some broadleaved trees have leaves with pointed ends so that rain drips off them easily.

How do trees grow?

Every year a tree grows taller. A layer or ring of new wood forms in the trunk and branches to make them stronger and thicker. The tree's roots grow and spread as the tree becomes heavier.

▶ This is a tree trunk cut in half. Each ring indicates one year of growth. This was a very old tree!

Tree Fact

Malaysia's acacia tree is the world's fastest-growing tree.

New growth also happens at the tips of the branches and twigs. Buds form on the twigs and split open to reveal new leaves.

▶ In spring, the leaves inside buds swell and the tree bursts into life.

15

How do trees make their own food?

Trees need air, water and sunlight to make their own food. A tree's leaves contain **chlorophyll**, the colouring which makes them green. Chlorophyll takes in energy from sunlight. Leaves use this energy to turn water from the ground and **carbon dioxide** from the air into a sugary liquid or **sap**. Sap is a tree's food.

veins

Tree Fact

The leaves of trees give off a gas called **oxygen**, which we need to breathe.

▲ The veins in this leaf are thin tubes that carry water and food.

▶ These buckets are collecting sap from this maple tree. We eat the sap as maple syrup.

A living home

Trees are home to many different plants and animals. Insects burrow into the bark looking for food and shelter. Birds make nests in trees and eat the insects and fruit they find there.

▼ This orchid lives in a tree. Its roots take in water from the air.

In tropical rainforests, snakes coil themselves around branches and monkeys swing from tree to tree. They sleep in nests they have made from fallen leaves.

▼ Cutting down
rainforest trees
destroys the homes
of creatures like
this orang-utan.

How do we use trees?

Trees give us food, building material and many other useful things. Many fruits, nuts and spices come from trees. **Latex**, the sap of rubber trees, is made into tyres and gloves.

▼ Wood from trees is used to make houses, furniture and flooring.

People use bark from some trees
to make beauty creams,
dyes and medicines.

Tree Fact

Without trees we would have
no wood and no paper, which
is made with crushed wood!

▲ It is important
that people plant new
trees to replace those
that are cut down.

Grow your own tree

See how a tree grows for yourself. Take a few pips from inside an apple. Soak the pips overnight in warm water. Plant the pips in a pot of damp soil. Make sure they are well covered. Seal the pot in a plastic bag and put it in a warm place. Keep a record of what happens as the seeds start to grow.

Tree Fact

Fruits that grow on trees include apples, cherries, mangoes, lemons and plums.

▲ Apple pips are the seeds of new apple trees.

22

▼ After this tree has blossomed, apples will begin to grow.

Glossary

bark
The outer covering that protects a tree trunk.

broadleaved tree
A tree with wide, flat leaves that produces flowers and fruit.

buds
Leaves and flowers form inside buds.

carbon dioxide
A gas in the air that trees use to make food.

chlorophyll
A substance in leaves that helps to make a tree's food.

cones
Cones grow around the seeds of conifer trees to protect them.

conifer
Trees with thin, spiny leaves. Conifers produce cones.

latex
The sap of rubber trees, used to make car tyres.

nutrients
Food in the soil that a tree needs to grow well.

oxygen
A gas that trees produce when they make food. People need to breathe oxygen to live.

palm tree
A tree with a slim trunk and waterproof leaves. Palm trees produce fruit.

roots
The parts of a tree that anchor it in the ground and take in water and nutrients from the soil.

sap
The sugary liquid trees make as food.

stem
The part of a plant that holds it upright.

tropical rainforests
Forests that grow in areas where it is hot and wet.

trunk
The woody stem of a tree, protected by bark.

Index